HAUS CURIOSITIES

Lion and Lamb

About the Author

MIHIR BOSE is an award-winning journalist and author who has written for the *Daily Telegraph* and *The Sunday Times*, and was the BBC's first sports editor. He has authored 30 books including *From Midnight to Glorious Morning?: India Since Independence* and *Silver: The Spy Who Fooled the Nazis*. Bose received an honorary doctorate from Loughborough University for his outstanding contribution to journalism and the promotion of equality.

Mihir Bose

LION AND LAMB

A Portrait of British Moral Duality

First published by Haus Publishing in 2018
4 Cinnamon Row
London SW11 3TW
www.hauspublishing.com

A CIP catalogue record for this book is
available from the British Library

Print ISBN: 978-1-912208-04-3
Ebook ISBN: 978-1-912208-03-6

Typeset in Garamond by MacGuru Ltd

Printed in Spain

To Priscilla, for her wonderful friendship
and enduring support

Contents

Acknowledgements

This book came about as a result of a conversation with Barbara Schwepcke, who thought it might make an addition to the Haus Curiosities series if I could persuade Lord Peter Hennessy, whose brainchild the series is. To my surprise and delight I could, and what is more I got a delightful lunch at the House of Lords. Following that, Harry Hall kindly agreed to give me a contract – maybe because I am, like him, a Tottenham sufferer. So, my thanks to Barbara, Peter and Harry. And to Jo Stimpson for her excellent editing. My thanks also to Jeremy Butterfield and to Rose Chisholm, without whose assistance the book would never have been completed. As usual, I cannot thank my wife, Caroline, enough.

A note on language
In the course of relating incidents of racially aggravated harassment, I have quoted statements using language that readers will find offensive. The publisher and I agree that the reproduction of this language is necessary to faithfully represent events as they occurred.

The lion and the ostrich

In the summer of 2014 my wife and I decided to have a short break in Yorkshire. I had been to Yorkshire often, but mostly on journalistic assignments to cities and towns. This would be a journey to the country. My wife, a proud country girl, feels I am too much of a townie, and this was a holiday to take me away from the city state of London, the modern Venice, and go for long walks through England's green and pleasant land. However, on one of our evening walks we got lost. My wife blamed me for not allowing her to bring the up-to-date Ordnance Survey maps. Fortunately, a farmer came by in his Land Rover and very kindly offered us a lift. After we had exchanged the usual pleasantries, the talk turned to farming and how farmers felt about government policies. With the 2015 elections coming up, and David Cameron having promised a referendum on the EU if he won, I was keen to find out how the farmer would vote. He readily conceded that Europe had been good for the farming community and that he received generous EU subsidies. But he said he would vote to leave.

The money did not matter. We needed, he said, to get control of our borders. There were far too many people flooding into this country; we just could not cope. Then he looked at me and said, "I can see you're from Sri Lanka." When I shook my head and said that, no, I had never even been to Sri Lanka, he said nothing and did not ask my country of origin.

Then, looking directly at me, he said, "I want my country back." With that he looked at my wife, who is white English, and smiled as if to say that she at least would understand why the natives of Britain felt this way. Away from London and metropolitan cities, in places where there are few non-whites, my wife is always extremely sensitive about how I am treated, but the farmer was not remotely hostile. We parted very amicably and returned to our hotel, where all the staff except one were from Eastern Europe. (The non-Eastern European one was from Australia, and about to get married to one of the Eastern Europeans.)

In the lead-up to the Brexit vote I often thought of the farmer and concluded that many, like him, might want their country back. I voted Remain but had a bet that the country would vote for Brexit. As a sports fan, I often bet against my favourite team – and such bets, which I hope I will lose, are meant to provide some monetary compensation should my team be defeated. The difference this time was that, unlike sporting encounters, the referendum was not the first leg of a two-legged football match, let alone the first Test of a five-Test series. There would be only one chance at the vote. Some Remainers may hope the House of Commons, or the various investigations into how the referendum was won, could make it otherwise, but what is taken for granted in sport is not possible in politics.

The farmer's cry, "I want my country back", also resonated with me because I have often heard similar cries, but on a football ground. Supporters unhappy with their manager and the board shout, "We want our club back!" But just as a football supporter has a mystical memory of the glories of his beloved team and cannot say which period of the club's history he wants to recreate, so the Leavers have until now failed to define which period of this country's vast and complex history they want to go back to. I do hope that none of them want a return to the 70s and 80s, when I was called a "Paki" and told to go back to Bangladesh (at that stage I had not visited either country). I often walked the streets in fear, and on a couple of occasions was worried I might not live to see another day. That has long passed. This is a different country, and I do not want that old country back.

I shall have more to say about immigration. Here let me say that I came from India nearly fifty years ago, not as a refugee or an economic migrant but because I was keen to become a writer. Indeed, in leaving India I gave up a privileged life which today would have seen me retire as a millionaire – while my writing, as my father warned me, has never made anything like that amount. However, it has given me much more pleasure than all the money I could have earned in India. In India, the only job I got was through nepotism, my family connections; here, I have been given opportunities not because anyone knows anything about my family – they do not – but because I have managed to convince media organisations and publishers that I have some ability. There have been enough good people judging me on what I can contribute rather than my skin colour.

Now, let me address the fact that what the Leavers are saying with their cry is that England should stop behaving like an ostrich and become a lion again. This is not a new cry, but one that has been heard regularly in this country since the end of the Second World War. The first time I heard it, it was certainly not uttered by a farmer, nor by anyone who would be classified as an ordinary working man, but by one of the country's leading intellectuals:

> The average Englishman [is] a much more attractive hybrid between a lion and an ostrich. In times of emergency he rises magnificently to the occasion. In between emergencies he buries his head in the sand with the tranquil conviction that reality is a nasty word invented by foreigners. This attitude is not only soothing, but also guarantees that a new emergency will soon arise and provide a new opportunity for turning into a lion and rising magnificently to the occasion.[1]

The writer went on to describe the British behaving like an ostrich over Munich but rising like a lion to defeat the Nazis, only for the ostrich to reappear after the war had been won and deprive "the lion of the fruit – or meat – of his victory". That writer was Arthur Koestler, and his version of the cry appeared in July 1963, in a special issue of *Encounter*, possibly the most influential literary journal at the time, entitled *Suicide of a Nation?: An Inquiry into the State of Britain Today*, which Koestler guest-edited. A Jewish-Hungarian refugee, who had managed to flee the Nazis and had arrived in the UK without an entry permit in 1940, Koestler was then at the height of his fame, a fame which was due in large measure to his having moved from communism to become a fervent Cold War warrior for the West. His novel *Darkness at Noon* showed how the best minds of the West could be seduced by communism and refuse to realise its evil nature.

Long before Nigel Farage, Koestler held the British political class responsible for turning victory into defeat:

> When the war was won, Britain's political and moral prestige in Europe was at an unprecedented height; in less than twenty years, her leaders managed to bring it down to an equally unprecedented low.[2]

The magazine was full of articles by the leading writers and thinkers of the day – Malcolm Muggeridge, Henry Fairlie, Cyril Connolly, Lord Altrincham (John Grigg) – all bemoaning the state of Britain. They depicted Britain in 1963 as a poor European outcast: its economy in desperate plight compared to those of France and Germany, which were booming thanks to the Common Market; its culture and education at a very low level; and its government reduced to begging President de Gaulle of France to let Britain join the European Economic Community, as it was then called.

Like many of the Leavers who can take a slice of history and present it as if it is the whole truth, Koestler and his fellow writers made no mention of the fact that, in winning the war, Britain had gone broke and its great economist, John Maynard Keynes, had had to rush to Washington in August 1945 to spend five months in hard negotiations – so hard, in fact, that the strain killed him shortly after – to persuade the Americans to provide a fifty-year loan, the final repayment of which was not made until 2006. The post-war years had seen bread and petrol rationed and, in 1947, potatoes as well. Three years after the war the US Air Force came back and acquired bases in this country which remain to this day.

I read the *Encounter* issue as a sixteen-year-old growing up in Mumbai, having found it while rummaging in the city's many street bookstalls. At that stage, Britain was held up to me as the ideal land without want, where every bedroom had an ensuite bathroom, every household had a cook and gardener and everyone dressed for dinner. That Britain's leading intellectuals now felt the country was ruined was a shock. (Interestingly, when I showed the front cover of that issue to friends after the EU vote, having concealed the date, all of them thought it was published after the referendum.)

This sense of despair was fairly widespread and reflected in the novels of that period. Five years after this supposed suicide, John le Carré published his novel *A Small Town in Germany*. The town he was referring to was Bonn, then the capital of West Germany. In the 60s le Carré had served as an intelligence official and diplomat in the British Embassy in Bonn, his job being to report on West German politics. He clearly drew on this experience to describe in the novel a fictional Germany where a former Nazi is emerging as a political leader, a sort of German Le Pen *avant la lettre*, who wants to put an end to the post-war Paris–Bonn axis and tilt West Germany towards Moscow. The British get alarmed, and one British diplomat sums up the situation thus:

> Here in Bonn we have at present one contribution to make: to maintain at all costs the trust and good will of the Federal Government. To stiffen their resolve against mounting criticism from their own electorate. The Coalition is sick; the most casual virus could kill it. Our job is to pamper the invalid. To console, encourage and

occasionally threaten him, and pray to God he survives long enough to see us into the Common Market... We are playing a poker game here. With open cards and nothing in our hand. Our credit is exhausted, our resources are nil... Our whole future with Europe could be decided in ten days from now.[3]

Le Carré could well have been writing about the feeling in the Foreign Office now. While Britain may have some cards to play, it is very far from a royal flush.

Yet it would be wrong to see this 60s debate of where the country is headed solely as a post-war, post-imperial phenomenon. It also went on in the middle of the Second World War, when there was no talk of the war resulting in the end of Empire; indeed, Winston Churchill famously declared that he had not become His Majesty's First Minister to preside over the liquidation of the Empire. It was against this background that George Orwell wrote *The Lion and the Unicorn*, calling for a revolution more dramatic than anything the Leavers have demanded. Orwell, undoubtedly the greatest English political writer of the 20th century, wrote the book during the Blitz and it was published in February 1941, four months before Hitler invaded Russia and ten months before the Japanese attack on Pearl Harbour brought the Americans in and made it truly a world war. At that stage, nobody could have predicted either event. Britain then seemed to be, as many in this country now like to portray it, a tiny island standing alone against the Nazis. In reality, it was the vast British Empire, covering a quarter of the globe, standing against the Nazis. However, there was no doubt that Hitler looked the most likely winner of this contest. Orwell argued that for Britain to upset the odds and beat Hitler there would have to be a political revolution:

> England is a family with the wrong members in control. Almost entirely we are governed by the rich, and by people who step into positions of command by right of birth. Few if any of these people are consciously treacherous, some of them are not even fools. But as a class they are quite incapable of leading us to victory.[4]

He highlighted how, in the third year of the war, England was still a "rich man's Paradise":

> All talk of 'equality of sacrifice' is nonsense... The bombed-out populations of the East End go hungry and homeless while wealthier victims simply step into their cars and flee to comfortable country houses... Even the rationing system is so arranged that it hits the poor all the time, while people with over £2,000 a year [£98,000 in today's money] are practically unaffected by it. Everywhere privilege is squandering good will.[5]

The subtitle of his essay was *Socialism and the English Genius*, and Orwell had no doubts about the virtues of that system. "Socialism," he wrote, "aims, ultimately, at a world-state of free and equal human beings. It takes the equality of human rights for granted."[6] Orwell outlined a six-point strategy for victory with the sort of nationalisation programme that even Jeremy Corbyn's most left-wing supporters would not propose: nationalisation of the land, mines, railways, banks and major industries; limitations of income; democratic reform of the educational system; an Imperial General Council "in which the coloured peoples are to be represented";[7] a formal alliance with China, Abyssinia and all other victims of the Fascist powers; and "immediate Dominion status for India, with power to secede when the war is over".[8]

But there was a catch. On India, Orwell went on to say:

What we must offer India is not 'freedom', which... is impossible, but alliance, partnership – in a word, equality. But we must also tell the Indians that they are free to secede, if they want to. Without that there can be no equality of partnership, and our claim to be defending the coloured peoples against fascism will never be believed. But it is a mistake to imagine that if the Indians were free to cut themselves adrift they would immediately do so. *When a British government offers them unconditional independence, they will refuse it. For as soon as they have the power to secede the chief reasons for doing so will have disappeared* [my italics].

A complete severance of the two countries would be a disaster for India no less than for England. Intelligent Indians know this. As things are at present, India not only cannot defend itself, it is hardly even capable of feeding itself. The whole administration of the country depends on a framework of experts (engineers, forest officers, railwaymen, soldiers, doctors) who are predominantly English and could not be replaced within five or ten years.[9]

Orwell also said, "In the age of the tank and the bombing plane, backward agricultural countries like India and the African colonies can no more be independent than can a cat or a dog."[10] Here the most eloquent anti-imperialist, who in this very book had written about Britain's "world-famed hypocrisy – their double-faced attitude towards the Empire",[11] sounded even more of an imperialist than Churchill. Not even Churchill, who in one of his speeches in the 30s had described the majority of Indians as "primitive people",[12] had gone quite so far. But Churchill never deviated from his view that India could never be given freedom, whereas Orwell wanted to have his cake and eat it: it was morally all right to promise Indians freedom because they would not accept it and nothing would change. Orwell's 1941 India policy is a perfect template for the Brexit scenario that the Leavers desire: withdraw from the EU, but still enjoy all the benefits of staying in.

Claiming the moral high ground

It has often fallen to foreigners to highlight the contradictions in such a stance. As George Santayana put it, "although he [the Englishman] is the most disliked of men the world over (except where people need some one they can trust) he is also the most imitated."[13] A more insightful explanation was provided by Pietro Quaroni, Italy's wartime ambassador in Afghanistan. In 1938, after much effort, he persuaded the British – who never liked foreign diplomats to visit their Indian colony – to allow him to travel from Kabul to Delhi. The British, being eternally fearful of foreign mischief, had the Italian closely followed. (So concerned were they about being caught unawares by Indians hostile to their rule that they had set up a special unit in London called the Indian Political Intelligence Office, the only one of its kind during imperial rule, and housed in the same building as MI5 and MI6. It was backed up by another intelligence operation in India, and the British ran such an extensive spying operation there that during the war the American consul in Mumbai warned, "Representatives of the United States Government in India should bear in mind at all times that they are functioning in a police state.")[14] Despite being watched, Quaroni got a good look at the British in India and concluded that they had two faces. There was the metropolitan face of Magna Carta, habeas corpus, the Mother of Parliaments and so forth, which only Westerners saw. But there was also, said Quaroni, the other face, the one the people in the East saw, the imperial face presented in the British colonies, "of how to rule and how to ensure obedience. With this second England, it is unwise to take liberties".[15] Orwell, writing about the metropolitan face, had been very eloquent:

> The gentleness of the English civilisation is perhaps its most marked characteristic. You notice it the instant you set foot on English soil. It is a land where the bus conductors are good-tempered and the policemen carry no revolvers. In no country inhabited by white men is it easier to shove people off the pavement.[16]

This was the world of *Dixon of Dock Green*, a very popular sitcom which ran until the 70s, depicting life in a London police station where petty crime was controlled through human understanding. Dixon, the police sergeant, valued common sense and would not have understood the need for the mailed fist of the imperial police.

The British have resolved this contradiction by never failing, even when they are behaving like rapacious lions and devouring all their enemies, to remind the world that deep down they are gentle lambs; should they ever err, they are quick to own up, or at least set up an inquiry to find out why the cuddly world of the lamb was suddenly shattered.

Nowhere was this better demonstrated than in the tribal areas between what was British India and Afghanistan, the region where the Taliban and jihadists today hold sway but where, at the height of the Raj, there were many tribes who refused to accept British rule. For them the British were not civilisers bringing progress, but oppressors. The greatest opponent of the Raj was the Faqir of Ipi, easily the most extraordinary guerrilla leader of the Second World War. Operating from his inaccessible hideouts in Waziristan he proved, says the historian Milan Hauner, "the most determined, implacable single adversary the British Raj in India had to face amongst its own subjects".[17] In order to deal with him the British maintained a large army on the North-West Frontier all through the war, used the Royal Air Force and Royal Indian Air Force to bomb villages and, not content with that, machine-gunned the inhabitants from armoured vehicles. They never captured him. But here we have a wonderful example of how the British are always keen to appear morally fair. White and red warning leaflets, a version of football's yellow and red cards, were dropped before the bombs rained down on the villages. Ironically, this British sense of fair play played into the Faqir's hands. The Faqir's followers believed he had divine powers. He had told them that he could turn British bombs into paper, and when the British leaflets came down from the air his followers required no further proof of his miraculous powers.

Over time the British even came to admire the Faqir. *The Times* upon his death in 1960 described him as "a doughty and honourable opponent", "a man of principle and saintliness" and "a redoubtable organizer of tribal warfare", and said that "many retired Army officers and political agents... will hear the news with the tribute of wistful regret".

It summed up how the British see themselves. They may use the most terrible means to subdue an enemy, but if he shows skill and valour the British will always admire him. Churchill himself exemplified this spirit. He fought his first war, what was called a "frontier war", in 1897, putting down a rebellion by Pathans in the Swat valley, now part of Pakistan. The war formed the subject of the first of his many books, *The Story of the Malakand Field Force*. The war was brutal, and the British burned rebel Pathan villages, which Churchill had no problems justifying:

> I invite the reader to examine the question of the legitimacy of village-burning for himself. A camp of a British brigade, moving at the order of the Indian Government and under the acquiescence of the people of the United Kingdom, is attacked at night. Several valuable and expensive officers, soldiers and transport animals are killed and wounded. The assailants retire to the hills. Thither it is impossible to follow them. They cannot be caught. They cannot be punished. Only one remedy remains – their property must be destroyed. Their villages are made hostages for their good behaviour. They are fully aware of this, and when they make an attack on a camp or convoy, they do it because they have considered the cost and think it worth while. Of course, it is cruel and barbarous, as is much else in war, but it is only an unphilosophic mind that will hold it legitimate to take a man's life, and illegitimate to destroy his property.[18]

Despite this, as he gazed down on the destroyed Mohmand villages and their trampled crops, he found much to admire in the Muslims:

It would be unjust and ungenerous to deny to the people of the Mamund Valley [the spelling then used] that reputation for courage, tactical skill and marksmanship, which they have so well deserved. During an indefinite period they had brawled and fought in the unpenetrated gloom of barbarism. At length they struck a blow at civilisation, and civilisation... will yet ungrudgingly admit that they are a brave and warlike race.[19]

The desire to be morally right also means the British have always been keen to punish those of their own citizens who have fallen from what they see as the highest moral standards, even when they honour these citizens. The classic example of this is Robert Clive. Visitors to King Charles Street in Whitehall can see a bronze statue of Clive and steps leading to the Foreign Office called Clive's Steps. It honours the fact that his victory at Plassey in June 1757 launched the Empire in India. Yet during Clive's life the British debated whether he should be punished for not observing the high moral standards this country sets itself.

At Plassey, Clive defeated Siraj ud-Daulah, the local Nawab, in what may be described as the military equivalent of cricket match fixing, a result arranged through judicious bribery of Mir Jaffar, Siraj's ambitious commander-in-chief. He was promised the kingship of Bengal in exchange for remaining neutral. At a crucial stage in the battle he did just that, and Clive won. But there was a second layer to Clive's intrigue: he also deceived a banker called Omichand who was the middleman in his deal with Mir Jaffar. Clive signed two treaties, the genuine one on white paper and a fictitious one on red which promised Omichand a lot of money that Clive had no intention of paying. Clive considered Omichand a rogue who deserved to be cheated and left unpaid. But even in this deception there was one British man of honour, Admiral Watson – he did not sign the counterfeit document, so Clive had to forge his signature.

In the years to come, after Clive returned home a very rich man, the British were troubled by how he had secured India, this jewel in the crown. There was a classic British Parliamentary inquiry producing voluminous reports, and Clive's conduct was debated in the House of Commons. The motion against Clive was proposed by Colonel Burgoyne, son-in-law of the Earl of Derby, who would later surrender to the Americans in Saratoga during their war of independence. He denounced Clive for his looting of Bengal and his deception of Omichand. Clive, defending himself, also staked a claim to the moral high ground, describing how, as he walked through Siraj's capital after his victory at Plassey, vaults "were thrown open to me alone, piled on either hand with gold and jewels. Mr Chairman, at this moment I stand astonished at my own moderation".[20] The debate perfectly illustrated the English duality of the lion also wanting to be the lamb. Part of Burgoyne's resolution, that Clive had made money, was accepted, but Clive was also praised for "great and meritorious services to this country".[21]

Clive's biographer Nirad Chaudhuri has written about this dilemma:

The plain issue was whether they could condemn Clive without condemning the very establishment of British power in India, which by the same moral standards that were at that moment being applied to Clive's conduct was naked aggression and usurpation, if not robbery... His misdeeds, if there were any in reality, were inconsequential and minor, compared with those of the Company. England could not retain the stolen goods if they called Clive a thief.[22]

Even if Clive's personal actions might have been ethically questionable, Britain could always point to the notorious Black Hole of Calcutta incident, which the British embraced as a very comforting moral blanket for all that happened in Bengal in the 18th century. There has been much historical debate about the incident. The story that outraged the British was that Siraj, after capturing Calcutta, imprisoned 146 Britons in a dreadful dungeon, and the next morning only 23 emerged alive. Historians have questioned whether Howell, one of the survivors, told the truth, in particular about how many were imprisoned. Moreover, as Jan Dalley has pointed out, the story is hardly one of "heroism and self-sacrifice to a cause".[23] The men involved had gone not in the name of any great national cause but to make money – and they (Howell included) made tons of it. But for the British, as Chaudhuri put it, "retrospectively, the Black Hole incident served to throw a moral halo over the British conquest of India, as if it was God's punishment for iniquity".[24]

This desire to show how the British are morally superior to all other people has, if anything, increased in recent years, as demonstrated by a comparison of how the Indian revolt of 1857 is narrated by British historians.

The revolt itself illustrated the two faces of Britain that Quaroni talked about. From the mid-19th century, British politicians mounted a campaign against atrocities committed by the Turkish Empire in the Balkans, with Gladstone leading the charge in his famous pamphlet *The Bulgarian Horrors and the Question of the East*. The British could grandstand on this high moral platform, despite the fact that in 1857 the British had outdone anything the Turks did in the Balkans. The most graphic illustration of this came during the 1857 revolt in which the British retook Delhi. Three Mughal princes, who had commanded the uprising in Delhi, were stripped naked and shot out of hand by Captain William Hodson. Hodson then stripped the corpses of their signet rings and armlets, pocketing these along with their bejewelled swords, and then wrote to his sister expressing pleasure at "the warm congratulations" he had received for "destroying the enemies of our race". "The whole nation will rejoice," he wrote.[25] It certainly did. Let us turn to Michael Edwards' book about the revolt, *The Red Year*. He mentions how Lord Canning, the Governor General, saw this – one of the most brutal acts in history – as "the first signal vengeance inflicted upon the foulest treason". But, writes Edwards:

> The signal vengeance was by no means over, nor was there any cessation in the amount of innocent blood ruthlessly shed, for the city of Delhi was put to the sword, looted and sacked with the ferocity of a Nazi extermination squad in occupied Poland.[26]

Edwards' book was published in 1973. Move forward to

2003 and we have Niall Ferguson's *Empire*. Ferguson has made his reputation as a historian of the right who believes that the British made the modern world and that the Empire was a force for good that ought to be celebrated. He describes a scene from 1857 just after the British had lifted the Siege of Lucknow. A young boy supporting a tottering old man approaches the gate of the city. The British officer, convinced that all Indians whatever their age must be rebels, brushes aside his plea for mercy and shoots the boy. Three times his revolver jams. The fourth time he succeeds, and then the boy falls. Ferguson, like Edwards, invokes the Nazis, but he adds a twist:

> To read this story is to be reminded of the way SS officers behaved towards Jews during the Second World War. Yet there is one difference. The British soldiers who witnessed this murder loudly condemned the officer's actions, at first crying 'shame' and giving vent to 'indignation and outcries' when the gun went off. It was seldom, if ever, that German soldiers in a similar situation openly criticized a superior.[27]

So, it is all right then. As long as one Briton protests against a massacre, the British can continue to claim the moral high ground. That historians have emerged in the 21st century arguing that we should all feel grateful about an empire which was a construct of the 19th century is not surprising. That sentiment chimes in with the popular view reflected in opinion polls that the empire was a force for moral good. It is as if they are counterbalancing the Rhodes

Must Fall movement and would like to make us believe that, contrary to whatever the evidence may show, the British ran their empire like a Victorian NGO, setting out to do good but occasionally, and understandably, lapsing.

England, my England

In the nearly fifty years I have lived here I have found much evidence of this lion–lamb duality. I was made very aware of it when I arrived in this country in January 1969 to study engineering at Loughborough University. Nine months earlier, Enoch Powell had made the infamous speech in which he fearfully expressed that observing the immigration of non-white people was "like watching a nation busily engaged in heaping up its own funeral pyre". He wrote, "As I look ahead, I am filled with foreboding; like the Roman, I seem to see 'the River Tiber foaming with much blood.'" He also quoted a white constituent telling him that he would not rest until all his children had emigrated, as he predicted that "in this country in 15 or 20 years' time the black man will have the whip hand over the white man".

While politicians condemned Powell, and he was sacked from the Tory Shadow Cabinet, opinion polls showed he reflected the popular mood. Dockers marched past Parliament in support of Powell, taunting a Sikh who was walking by. I was much taken by a photograph of a black man walking past a wall which carried the graffiti "Enoch for PM". Michael Heseltine would later say that Powell could have been elected Prime Minister by an overwhelming majority.

There was one part of Powell's speech which had particular relevance to me. He had argued that the only solution

for the River Tiber not to foam with blood was to repatri-
ate people of colour back to their countries of origin. He
described "the urgency of implementing now the second
element of the Conservative Party's policy: the encouragement of re-emigration".

So, I arrived not knowing whether I would be sent home.
My first few weeks were certainly worrying. About two
weeks after I arrived in Loughborough, while walking in the
town one day, I got into a conversation with a middle-aged
lady. She asked me where I was from, and when I told her I
was from India she smiled and said, "Young man, you speak
English very well. Obviously, you have been well educated in
our country. I hope you will go back to your homeland soon
and use it to improve your country. It requires people like you
trained in this country." It was not difficult to believe that this
lady wanted Powell's repatriation policy to be implemented.

Yet within six weeks of arriving I had not been sent home,
and was instead being encouraged to stand for election as
President of the Students' Union. I had made my reputation as a wit when, in a debate about the awful food in our
hall, I had said, "In India I was told the Irish liked potatoes.
I did not know the English also liked them." Back in 1969
you could make such a joke without being considered a racist.
But while there was support for me, for a fresher to win was
unheard of, and during the campaign one student in his final
year patted me patronisingly on the back and said, "Your
time will come, but not now. First learn about the place and
us." On the day of the election it snowed. I had never seen
snow before and I wondered if many would bother to vote,
especially as it was for a "coloured" man they knew nothing

about. But, to my great surprise, many students did vote. I won, and won easily. Later, a young female student who had been at the university for a couple of years said, "I voted for that man because he seems honest. Looking at his face I feel he won't run away with the cash." She could not have known many non-whites – there were probably, including me, only about a dozen at the university – but she was clearly happy to let this "coloured" man have the whip hand, albeit only over the Students' Union.

But while the university sheltered me against any racial discrimination, in my early years in London in the 60s and 70s – a very different London to the one I live in now – I was made very aware of my race. It started when, having decided to qualify as a chartered accountant, I went for an interview with the senior partner of an accountancy firm. After he had grilled me, and just as we were about to part, he told me, "Well, I hope you will live in an area where there are not too many Indians. The trouble with Indians is that they tend to congregate together." Then he added, "Oh, by the way, you can get a student edition of *The Times*." So, I turned to *The Times* to look for accommodation. The paper was unlikely to have many places in Southall, which already by then was known as "mini-India", and I had a choice of many other London places where Indians did not "congregate together". The hunt for a flat always started with a very friendly telephone conversation, at the end of which I would be invited to view the property. But the moment I rang the doorbell, the lady who opened the door (it was generally a lady, and rather an old one at that) would invariably say, "I am sorry, I have just let the flat." After many such rejections I began to wonder if it would not be better to warn the next landlady that I was from India. So, when one day I saw an attractive advertisement in *The Times* about a place in Hampstead, after the (by now) very pleasant conversation and the landlady having said she would be delighted for me to come over and have a look, I added, "Oh, by the way, I am an Indian." For a few seconds there was silence and then I heard, "I am dreadfully sorry, but my husband would not like that."

My experiences made me turn to writers like James Baldwin, Eldridge Cleaver, Frantz Fanon and VS Naipaul to understand the non-white experience, and led me to change my sporting allegiance. I had grown up in India worshipping Australian cricket. They were not only some of the most gifted cricketers in the world, they also sent their best teams to India when England sent B-teams – many of whom, including the captains, had never even played for England. The result was that, except when Australia played India, we all supported Australia. This was most marked when Australia played the West Indies. There was, of course, a huge contradiction in this. Australia had a White Australia policy, and ran an assisted migration policy under which white Britons could emigrate to Australia for just ten pounds (its beneficiaries were known colloquially as "ten-pound Poms"), while making it well-nigh impossible for Indians to settle in Australia. We did not know any of this, and even if we had, I am not sure it would have diminished our affection for the country.

After a few months in England, aware that my colour mattered, I switched to supporting the West Indies when they played Australia. My moment of conversion came when an Englishman, discussing a Test in which the West Indies were doing well, said, "You must be very happy, your team is doing well." Listening to the man, I realised that my dark skin meant he would always see me as supporting another dark-skinned person. I thought back to my school days, when I was totally unaware of what skin colour represented, so much so that I had rooted for the Swedish boxer Ingemar Johansson in 1961. He fought the black American Floyd Patterson for the world heavyweight title, and I was devastated when the blonde Swede lost. However, by 1970, after two years in this country, I could see that – whether I liked it or not – in Britain I was a person of colour and would always be seen as representative of so-called "coloured" people. This made me seek out those who were champions of this world, and an obvious hero was Muhammad Ali. I was devastated when in 1971 Ali lost to Joe Frazier. Aware of my colour as I was by then, I felt that Ali was fighting for us, and his defeat was our defeat. Five years later, in 1975, I wrote about my experiences in England and described myself as a "marginal man", borrowing the expression from a Jewish friend of mine who felt the same way about life in this country.

I have long shed that feeling, and have even got round the problem that my name posed for the English (and still does). Afua Hirsch, the writer and broadcaster, says in her book *Brit(ish): On Race, Identity and Belonging*, "I cannot pronounce my name... Thirty-five years into bearing this name, I have failed to master it."[28] Hirsch is of mixed British-Ghanaian heritage and is talking of how Ghana's five centuries of mingling with Britain have meant that "Britain is now littered with people like me; Ghanaians – many high-profile – who either mispronounce their names or give in to other people doing it for them".[29] She was born long after I settled in this country, but like her I was aware that my name caused problems, and even taking an English-sounding name could be difficult. During the summer holidays in 1969 I worked in a factory in Leicester. Realising my name would be a problem, I suggested to the foreman that he call me Mick. As he introduced me to his fellow workers he said, "Well, this is Mick. He is going to be working with us from today." A large, fat, barrel-chested man wearing a blue apron looked hard at me and then said, "Bloody hell, we've now got a coloured Irishman, have we?" And at this everyone laughed. After I became a journalist I did write articles under the pen name of Michael Bevington and even David Sterling – the second appropriate enough, thought the editor, for a financial column – but that was what in journalism is called using a "cod name". (What this means is that a paper allows a journalist to write for a rival publication but does not allow him or her to write under their own name. It is a common practice in the profession.) Name-change amongst Indians is not unknown. I know Sunils who have become Neils, and the very successful businessman Nathuram Puri shortened his first name to Nat, as he found Nathuram was imposing too big a burden on the English. My father had named me after a 6th-century Indian astronomer, mathematician and astrologer. I decided I would not change my name. And here the *Sunday Times* copytakers gave me an idea.

In the 70s, long before the age of emails, it was common to telephone copy in. But the first time I telephoned the copytaker and gave my name, he was very puzzled. To him Mihir sounded like I was saying "me here". He asked, "Yes, I know you are there, but who are you? What is your name?" I had to spell out my name, and this became a regular thing when giving copy. The process was made more difficult by the fact that I was often doing this from a football ground against a background of some sixty thousand fans shouting the place down. But it worked, and after my first football match report for the paper where my name was misspelt, there were no problems. The copytaker's "me here" set me thinking, and I decided that was the way to get the English to accept Mihir and not make me a "coloured Mick". So, when I introduced myself thereafter I said, "I am sorry, I have a difficult name. You say 'me here' and I say 'I am here'." It has never failed to produce a laugh. Now when I hear football supporters taunting opposing teams who are not playing well by singing "Who are you?", I think of *Sunday Times* copytakers, who should claim copyright for that song.

This may be seen as the soft, witty side of British accept-ance. The two really crucial moments when I saw both the face of the rapacious, bloodthirsty British lion and the cuddly, loveable lamb also involved *The Sunday Times* and took place within a few months of each other in 1981.

The 80s were a time when football was going through massive changes, not all of them welcome, which eventu-ally led to the birth of the Premier League. There was vio-lence both inside and outside the grounds. On match days at railway stations there would now be policemen in the forecourt, complete with dogs, making sure the away fans travelling to the football match did not cause any problems. When these fans got to their destination, they were treated like a foreign army, met off the trains by policemen with dogs, who escorted the away supporters to the ground. The pylons carrying the floodlights had once been the indicators of a ground's location, acting as a sort of makeshift but unerring GPS. Now on match days it was the sight of police vans and dogs waiting some distance from the ground that was a much more conspicuous indicator. What made it worse was that, in order to cope with the violence on the terraces, football turned back to a policy that society at large considered immoral. By the 70s segregation in public life because of colour had been banned; even those advertisements outside boarding houses saying "no dogs, no coloured, no Irish" had disappeared. Now, in football, segregation was reintroduced on the basis of which team a fan supported, with separate entrances for home and away fans. As supporters approached a ground they had to declare their tribal allegiance. "Home or away?" asked the stewards to help them direct the fans to the correct safe enclosure. And I no longer needed the referee to start glancing at his watch to be aware that the match was nearing its end. A few minutes before the finish, the public address system would warn the away supporters to stay in their enclosure until the police had cleared the ground of home supporters. Then and only then would they be escorted back to their coaches or the railway station. To the everlasting shame of football in this country, this practice continues to this day, and fans see it as so normal that when there is violence it is blamed on not having segregation.

The 70s and 80s also saw the emergence of black players, but the crowds watching them were almost all white, and many made it clear they did not like blacks playing football. There would be monkey chants every time a black player touched a ball, often bananas and other objects would be thrown at them and players would even be spat at. When John Barnes played for Liverpool, the Everton supporters regularly chanted "Niggerpool, Niggerpool, Niggerpool," while also declaiming, "Everton are white, Everton are white." And when Barnes scored a wonderful goal for England against Brazil in the Maracanã, Brazil's historic stadium and an iconic venue in world football, some English football supporters said it did not count as an England goal because he was black.

Then, English football press boxes were uniformly white; I hardly saw a non-white face at the ground anywhere, and the odd football manager would look hard at me if I asked a question. Once, at a match between Luton and Southampton, the Southampton manager, Lawrie McMenemy, having seen his team lose, was upset by a question I asked. He turned on me and said, "What match were you at, pal? Are you sure you're not at the wrong type of game? This is football, pal." My fellow journalists were quick to laugh at my expense. The following week, Luton were due to play Liverpool – then in their pomp. Southampton had got a 1–1 draw there, and McMenemy was asked what advice he would give Luton. He answered, "Go to church and pray before the match." Then he turned to me and said, "I don't know where you would go to pray, pal." With that, this giant Coldstream Guardsman strode out of the press room, while my fellow hacks fell about in merriment. The only person upset was the Luton manager, David Pleat, who almost felt he had to apologise on behalf of the managers' union. McMenemy could not have chosen a more curious place to make such a comment about prayer, given the setting of the Luton ground. The nearby streets had impeccable English names like Oak Street and Beech Street, yet the houses were occupied by Muslims from Kashmir and Bangladesh. That day, my car had been parked next to a shop called Kashmir Stores, where the shopkeeper, with his russet-coloured hair and mullah's beard, looked more at home with the basket of pistachios next to his counter than with the Yorkies he was selling. On either side of the road I could see women with their heads covered – the word "hijab" had not become fashionable, and they were generally called "shawls" – accompanied by little boys, slowly making their way home. They could have been in Mirpur or Sylhet for all the notice they took of Luton Town Football Club. If McMenemy had asked these people, "Where do you pray, pal?" they would have thought him an imbecile. Even in the gathering gloom of that autumn evening, I could see the minarets of three mosques surrounding the ground. All I can suppose is that McMenemy had not glanced out of the team coach as it swung into the Kenilworth Road car park, and had not realised how immigration had changed Britain.

But for me McMenemy's comments did not matter. I took my cue from the *Sunday Times* football correspondent, the novelist and playwright Brian Glanville. He had drummed into me that it was not worth listening to what football managers said. Readers wanted the opinion of the reporter, not the post-match rantings of managers.

But then came two incidents in 1981, when I realised I could not ignore the dark side of football. The first was towards the end of the 1980–81 football season, when I was on my way to Norwich to cover the game against Arsenal. I travelled to the match feeling full of myself. I had persuaded

John Lovesey, the sports editor of *The Sunday Times*, that this would be a suitable opportunity for an experiment in reporting. An article in *Time Out* had said that most journalists and directors watched football from a seat in line with the centre circle rather than watching from behind the goal as the terrace supporters did. This, said the writer, gave them a middle-class bias as opposed to representing the supposedly more genuine working-class view from behind the goalposts. It was, of course, nonsense – but it gave me an idea. I suggested to Lovesey that we send not one but five reporters to a match. Get one to stand with the hardcore terrace supporters, another with the manager in the dugout, a third with the chairman and a fourth with the season ticket holders in the main stand. These four journalists would report the match through the eyes of their chosen subjects. In addition, there would be the normal match reporter sitting in the press box to provide the usual match report. The whole exercise would indicate whether a person's view of the match changes because of where he is watching it from.

Lovesey was attracted to the idea, and I was given the task of sitting in the directors' box with the Norwich chairman at the time, Sir Arthur South. As I made my way to the entrance marked "Directors", I heard a cry: "Get your copy of the *Bulldog*, get your colour supplement!" I turned to see a man with close-cropped hair and a bomber jacket bearing the National Front insignia on its arm, selling copies of a newspaper. I soon forgot about him as I tried to portray the match through Sir Arthur South's eyes. He had cheerfully confessed he did not know anything about football, but he knew men, and that enabled him to judge how the team was performing. I had thought the *Time Out* writer was talking pretentious rubbish until I was invited to the Norwich directors' box. I had not realised how class-ridden football clubs could be. It was a world removed from the pen where the away supporters were herded. Here there was no frisking, no injunction to wait until the home supporters had left. The style and opulence of the hospitality available to directors and their guests surprised me. I was ushered into the board-room for a pre-match drink, and at half-time there was a magnificent spread supplemented by as much free drink as I could manage. I also for the first time at a football match saw a certain kind of well-heeled woman in expensive furs, wearing tasteful but costly jewellery with what looked like a permanent suntan. Many years later I learned that the tan was very often acquired through hours in a sunbed rather than actual exposure to the sun.

I was full of these thoughts when, after the match, I along with my *Sunday Times* colleagues rushed to get the train back to London. We reached the station just as the London train was pulling out, and jumped in the first available compart-ment just as the train left. It was then, as I walked down the aisles towards first class, that I realised I had got in at the back of the train packed with Arsenal supporters returning to London. They should have been in a good mood, their team having won 1–0, but, far from being happy, they seemed very angry. As I walked past them they looked at me with faces like thunder. As I went past one particularly large supporter, he looked at me and cried out, "Coon, coon, hit the coon over the head with a baseball bat." Then he got up and started fol-lowing me. It was extremely fortunate that by the time he did so I had gained some distance on him, and a couple of people had interposed themselves, quite unwittingly, between the two of us. But this seemed only to add to his sense of urgency to hit the "coon".

So, as we sped away from Norwich, a strange procession made its way through the train: me, buffeted between two of my *Sunday Times* colleagues, and behind us this fat Arsenal supporter crying out, "Coon, coon, hit the coon over the head with a baseball bat". I had never heard this song before. It was only later that I learned it was a very popular football song. I quickened my step, but I could not really make a run for it. I was going through some very crowded compartments and they were all filled with hard-faced young men who looked angry and menacing. As the cries of "Coon, coon, hit the coon over the head with a baseball bat" grew nearer and louder, I feared that the Arsenal supporters in the rows we were passing through would take up the chant and reach out for me. It was clearly intended as an incitement to provoke such an assault on me, but fortunately for me they didn't take the bait. Then, just as the instigator brushed past one of my colleagues and reached for me, I stepped into the first-class carriage. And the first person both of us saw sitting there was a policeman – a black policeman.

This was one "coon" he could not trifle with. Now, as the policeman put himself between me and the supporter, the situation was completely transformed. The supporter's cries died as if someone had switched off the power, and when the policeman started to question him he looked more than a little confused.

Once the policeman had apprehended the "coon"-basher,

I was quite prepared to let the matter rest. But one of my *Sunday Times* colleagues, a tough Irish-born journalist who had reported on the Troubles in Ireland, was most outraged by what had happened and insisted I bring charges. I eventually agreed. My colleague rang the office – in those days before mobile phones we had to wait until we got to Liverpool Street – and then decided that we ought to recover in a fish restaurant in Soho that he knew well. So, over champagne and oysters, we put the incident behind us.

It was winter of 1981 by the time the case came to court, and my colleague and I returned to Norwich to provide evidence. I had doubts about the journey. Would the aggressor be on the train? Would he have with him his mates, who might complete the job he had been so keen on in the spring? But I need not have feared. This midweek journey in the pale winter sunshine could not have been more different to the one on that spring evening. If he was on the train, we did not see him. At Norwich we were met by a very friendly policeman who epitomised the best in English policing.

When I finally saw the Arsenal supporter in court he could not have looked more different to the frightening vision I had carried of him since that train ride. Now, instead of jeans and a T-shirt he wore a suit; his disorderly hair was slicked down as if he had washed it but not dried it; and he looked like an unremarkable if rather overweight young man. It turned out he was a chef who was not always in work, and his story, as told to the Norwich court, was a sad one, made all the more pitiable by his extreme contrition. He had got into bad company, but now he had straightened himself out, and such behaviour would not happen again. His guilty plea meant we did not have to give evidence, and he was fined £20 for abusive language and threatening behaviour.

Before I arrived at the courtroom, I had been apprehensive about how I would feel when confronting him again. On that crowded train full of Arsenal supporters, in the middle of his tribe, he had looked like an ogre, with me rendered the alien. Now he was the outsider, in surroundings that to me were part of the reassuring correction system necessary in a civilised society. On the train he had behaved as if he were the butcher and I a mere sacrificial lamb waiting for the slaughter. Now, in the courtroom, he seemed to be going through such a terrifying sense of bewilderment that I actually felt sorry for him. He was clearly intimidated by the court, the judge, the lawyers in their wigs. When he apologised and promised never to stray again, I almost felt like patting him on the back and saying "there, there". I did not, but I felt both removed from his world and not a little contemptuous of his background and upbringing. The difference was emphasised when, at the end of the hearing, he slunk away, unable to meet my eyes, while my colleague and I went with the policeman for a very civil lunch and then a leisurely return home to London.

Years later I was to read in Bill Buford's book *Among the Thugs* about his experience of football violence on a train coming back from Wales. A drunken supporter got into a first-class carriage and tried to set fire to a well-dressed man whose clothes and manner indicated his wealth. Buford depicted it as "a telling image: one of the disenfranchised, flouting the codes of civilized conduct, casually setting a member of a more privileged class alight".

On the train back to Liverpool Street my colleague plied me with drinks, and that midweek evening train ride was a marvellous contrast to the journey back from the Arsenal match. Just as almost everything surrounding that train ride had been a nightmare, now everything was reassuring, from the gathering autumnal mist which allowed us fleeting glimpses of the passing East Anglian countryside to the elegantly dressed businessmen and women, so perfectly behaved, thoughtful and polite not only to each other but also to strangers. I could imagine them all being *Archers* listeners and saying "sorry" all the time. This was just the England I had always imagined. By the time the train arrived at Liverpool Street, the sometime-employed chef was like a Victorian cartoon villain, little connected with my everyday world. I may have glimpsed Caliban on the train back from the Norwich–Arsenal match but now, six months later, Camelot had re-emerged, and everything was all right with the world.

Three weeks later, I was on the 19:03 train from Nottingham, having covered Nottingham Forest playing against Leeds, and I was back in the world far removed from the magical Camelot I had been brought up to believe England was. The train had six first-class compartments at the front. They were completely deserted, but this did not worry me. I quite liked the solitude. I had Arthur M. Schlesinger's biography of Robert Kennedy, which had accompanied me on my football travels that season, and there were newspapers available, including the sporting pink. I settled down to read, quite happy to be on my own. It was some time after the train had left Nottingham that I became aware that I had every reason to be very worried.

The first sign was a series of shouts and cries in the corridor leading to the compartments. Soon I found a boy – he could not have been more than twelve – pressing his face against the door of the compartment and flattening his nose against the glass in racial ridicule. He was joined by a second who shouted "Sieg Heil", and then started marching up and down the corridor. A few minutes later there were more boys – four of them in all – and they slid open the door of my compartment and entered. They introduced themselves as trainspotters. One of them, a chubby boy who wore plimsolls, resembled, apart from his colour, my own features at that age. He did most of the talking.

Who was I, what did I do, he asked.

When I told him I was a sports reporter, he exchanged a look with his friends and then said, "How do you know anything about football? Pakis don't know anything about football, do they? Who do you work for?"

"*Sunday Times*," I said. This seemed to throw them, and I got the impression that *The Sunday Times* was not a paper the boys were familiar with.

"What's your name?" asked the chubby boy. When I told him he said, "What? Not Patel? All you Pakis are called Patel. That's what the Paki who owns the corner shop is called. What do you think of the National Front?" When I made no response he asked, "What do you think of Enoch Powell?"

"I understand he is a very fine Greek scholar." This reply seemed to throw them, and silence reigned for a few minutes during which I thought that Powell's 1968 speech still echoed. The boy could not have been born when Powell made it.

My thoughts were interrupted by the chubby boy, who

had noticed my sporting pink and asked whether I knew the Manchester United score. He was, he said, a United supporter. I extended the paper to him.

He looked at it. "2–1 to United," he said happily. But then his face contorted into a scowl. "That wog Moses scored again." Moses was a player of mixed race.

For a time, they left me in peace and even went away from the compartment. But soon they returned, and now there was a different mood. They no longer wanted to chat; they were acting as my well-wishers, out to warn me of the dangers ahead.

The chubby boy came in and said, "There's a bunch of hooligans in the next compartment. Chelsea supporters. They are not in a happy mood." Chelsea were then in the Second Division and that day they had lost 6–0 to Rotherham. I was aware of the reputation of Chelsea fans and feared the worst.

The boys seemed to sense this and began to play on my fears. For what seemed like ages, but was probably no more than fifteen minutes, they came in and out of my compartment warning me of the hooligans in the next one and the dangers that lay in store for me. The train was now passing stations familiar to me from my university days at Loughborough. Back then, the station names were for me reassuring landmarks on a journey so pleasant and relaxing I would be glad not to have reached my destination yet. Now I desperately peered through the darkness hoping against hope that I would see signs for London St Pancras.

Just before Wellingborough the boys returned, and the chubby one said, "They're going to get you before St Pancras. We're getting off at Wellingborough." Then, with a smile which suggested he had tried to play the good Samaritan but could do no more to help me, he and his friends were off. As the train left Wellingborough I decided to take what precaution I could, and put on my coat and muffler. I opened and reopened the Kennedy book, shuffled the pages of the newspaper, but could not concentrate on the words. I dared not look into the corridor, aware that my nemesis was supposed to come from there.

Just as the train departed Luton the lights went off, plunging my compartment into utter darkness. I thought this was an accident. I later learned that there were switches in the train which determined people could get at and use to plunge the train into darkness, and that the Chelsea hooligans had undoubtedly done so.

I flicked on my lighter and checked my watch, praying for the minute hand to move faster and St Pancras to come. Just then, the lights came back on, and as they did the long-threatened Chelsea mob finally arrived. There were about ten of them, their blue-and-white scarves flaunted across their persons. The leader was a man dressed in a woolly red jumper. He theatrically flung open the door of the compartment and, dancing in front of me as if in a war dance, seized me by my lapels and pulled me out of my seat.

"He's mine," he cried. Then, pressing his face close to me, he said, "OK, mate, this is a mugging."

As if on cue, the lights in the carriage began flickering on and off, and as the train plunged in and out of tunnels there were brief spasms of light followed by utter darkness. By now the mates of the jumper-wearing man who had claimed me had crowded into the compartment, some of them, like him, doing a war dance and jumping up and down on the seats in front of me. Their faces were contorted in mocking, hateful, grimaces. One stood in front of me and started to shadow-box silently; another pushed me about. They all disputed the right to work over what they called "the wog".

The man in the jumper pushed me away, and as I sank back to my seat he grabbed my briefcase and scattered the contents round the compartment with a triumphant shout. Another one snatched the lighter from my hand and smashed it against one of the walls, while another grabbed my cigars and yet another asked for my wallet, but then seemed to lose interest and started jumping up and down in front of me. All the while, they talked amongst themselves. Who did "the wog" belong to? Who would have him? Who would make the kill? I was now surrounded on all sides by the Chelsea army and felt like a missionary tied before the fire while the natives danced around me. I could feel the flames licking me and it seemed it was only a matter of time before I was tossed into them.

I did genuinely feel that I might not live through this situation, and my mind seemed to dwell on curious, irrational things. For that day's match I had changed the way I took notes, particularly on the precious team formation of which *The Sunday Times* was so fond. Had this, I wondered quite stupidly, disturbed the traditional pattern, altered the cosmic waves around me and brought about this unexpected retribution? I also thought of the pair of gloves I had left in the driving compartment of my car in London, a natty pair that I usually carried in the outer pocket of my overcoat. Now I had a vision that, after they found my body, they would go to my car and unearth the gloves. The story would be headlined "The Man Who Left His Gloves Behind".

Suddenly, just when it seemed the Chelsea mob had made up its mind and was ready to roast me, a cry went up: "Old Bill's coming." The train was slowing down in its approach to St Pancras. A lookout had noticed that the Transport Police had started boarding the train as it entered the station and, as if by magic, the Chelsea mob forgot about me and vanished. I feared it might be a false reprieve, but to my great relief I realised the train was pulling into the platform. I slowly gathered myself and my things, and made my way out. As I did so, I noticed that a fire was burning in a toilet behind me.

As with the Norwich experience, once again the justice system of this country had come to my rescue. But it was what followed that emphasised to me the lion–lamb duality of Britain. My initial reaction was to resolve that I would give up football reporting. Lovesey would not hear of it, and decided that this was a story *The Sunday Times* should feature. He assigned Dudley Doust, the sports feature writer, to it. Doust, an American, was famous for the way in which he teased details from the person he was writing about – the joke at *The Sunday Times* was that my suffering at the hands of the Chelsea mob was nothing compared to what Doust was going to put me through. Sure enough, over the next few days Doust rang me at least a dozen times, possibly more. No fact was too unimportant, no detail too inconsequential. He spoke to me at length about my leaving the gloves in my car compartment and what this meant. But the article he produced, "Journey into Terror on the 19:03 from Nottingham", was a masterpiece of re-creation. Lovesey ran it as the lead item on the sports feature page, although some journalists felt it should have been on the front page. The article produced an incredible reaction. Apart from one woman who said the reason for the attack was not race but class, as the Chelsea fans were incensed I was travelling in first class, I was inundated with letters both deploring the incident and expressing outrage and sympathy. It made me decide I would not give up football reporting, although for almost five years after that, until the beginning of the 1985 season, I avoided trains and drove to matches, even if it meant driving up to Swansea and back in a day. I also now planned my football trips as if I were a general preparing for battle. Whatever match I was covering, I always checked where teams like Chelsea, West Ham and Leeds – whose fans had a reputation for violence – were playing, and took detours to avoid their possible paths. I always went very early, often arriving at the town some three hours before the match and driving up to the ground even before the stewards had arrived. Sometimes I had to wait until they unlocked the gates. But I knew that by getting in so early I could park my car as near to the ground as possible. My objective was to cut down the distance I had to travel from the ground to my car after the match. I saw my car as the armoured truck which could speed me away from trouble. What sustained me was not only the support of *The Sunday Times* and that of my many friends, but the evidence I had from wider English society that the football fans who had waved the Gatling gun in my face were vastly outnumbered by people whose behaviour had made Orwell talk of "the gentleness of the English civilisation".[30] This was still a country where "sorry" was the most often-repeated word, and the most used phrase when a person misbehaved was "you are so silly".

The postscript to this was that, sometime after, I got Enoch Powell to review a book for me for a magazine I was editing. I did not, of course, refer to the chubby boy, but I did wonder what the boy would have made of my very amicable exchange with Powell. The book was on Germany being the first country to have social insurance, and Powell was both erudite and very readable. I regret now that I did not try and meet him, because I would have liked to know what he would have made of the chubby boy.

The perils of having one's cake and eating it

Powell's speech, of course, was a classic case of trying to have it both ways: making a racist and highly immoral speech, but presenting it in the most moral terms. To his dying day Powell claimed he had spoken not about race but immigration, yet his speech was spattered with stories from constituents who were racist. Powell, as Matthew Parris has pointed out, was using these stories to "disguise but not entirely conceal his racism". So, he quoted a letter he had received from a white widow saying that black immigrants had pushed excreta through her letter box and that "wide-grinning piccaninnies" who could not speak English followed her down the street calling her "racialist".[31] Powell emphasised that he himself was not saying all this, but merely reporting what his constituents had told him, and that as a Member of Parliament it was his duty to address their concerns.

But perhaps his cleverest manoeuvre was to portray the Race Relations Bill that the Labour government was piloting through Parliament as prejudiced. The proposed legislation banned discrimination in public places. Powell argued that this was "a one-way privilege" directed at the white majority and "enacted to give the stranger, the disgruntled and the agent-provocateur the power to pillory [the native white population] for their private actions."[32] Even when he asked for immigrants to be sent home, he made sure he was safely mounted on his moral high horse. One of the main thrusts of his speech was that dependants of non-white immigrants who were already here were being allowed to flood into the country. He wanted that stopped immediately. Not that he wanted families divided, of course. But, he said, families should be united in their countries of origin, as "suspension of immigration and encouragement of re-emigration hang together, logically and humanly".[33]

Powell's misuse of intellectual respectability to cloak his racism must be contrasted with the behaviour of a fellow Tory just before Powell's infamous speech. That politician was Iain Macleod, and his honourable intervention came when in 1968 the Labour government of Harold Wilson rushed through the Commonwealth Immigrants Act 1968, popularly known as the Kenyan Asians Bill, a piece of legislation which Tony Benn described as the most shameful piece of legislation the Commons had ever passed. The legislation went back on the pledge given by a previous Conservative government that people from the Indian subcontinent who had been brought to Kenya as "coolie" labourers would, after Kenya became free, find a home in Britain should they be thrown out. Macleod, who as Colonial Secretary had negotiated the deal, was one of the few major politicians to speak out against the Bill, saying that he had given his word, that he meant to give it and that what was happening now was wrong. Macleod knew that in taking this stance he was going against the policy of his Shadow Cabinet and destroying whatever small chance he had of being leader of the Conservatives. But, unlike Powell, Macleod was not trying to have his cake and eat it.

Nothing better illustrates the British desire to have their cake and eat it than the emergence of the modern Commonwealth. The British, like all the European democracies – including the French and the Dutch – went to the Second World War fighting for freedom, but with no intention of giving freedom to their colonial subjects, an attitude that Orwell paraphrased as "not counting niggers".[34] But Japan's victory over the European powers in Asia destroyed the mystique of the European. The British understood, as the French and the Dutch did not, that it was not worth fighting ruinous wars to preserve their Asian empires. The end of the Second World War saw mutinies by Indian soldiers, and in Mumbai virtually the entire Indian navy mutinied. After six years of war, British soldiers were not prepared to go to India to subjugate Indians. A popular song among demob-happy British soldiers in India went:

Land of shit and filth and wogs,
Gonorrhoea, syphilis, clap and pox,
Memsahibs' paradise, soldiers' hell,
India, fare thee fucking well.

As Labour Chancellor Hugh Dalton put it, "When you are in a place where you are not wanted, where you have not the force to squash those who don't want you, the only thing to do is come out".[35] Yet even as the British withdrew from India they wanted to hold on to the country like a nanny holding on to a child, showing how very sentimental the British can be. Indian independence in 1947 and the simultaneous creation of Pakistan posed a problem the British had never faced before. India and Pakistan were the first non-white dominions to become self-governing. Before 1947 the only such dominions were majority-white countries: Australia, New Zealand, Canada and South Africa. The "white" dominions accepted the King as their head of state, whose representative in their country was called the Governor-General. The Indians, however, saw dominion status as a temporary measure until they finalised their constitution and became a republic, ending formal ties with the British Crown.

But the British just could not bear to cut ties with India. Clement Attlee wrote to Jawaharlal Nehru, India's Prime Minister. Having never thought parliamentary democracy could work in India, Attlee wanted India's constitution to have a specific role for the British monarch. He wondered if a republic was really in the traditions of India, and suggested a title might be found for the King from India's heroic age. He talked about the royal family being of a universal nature, transcending creeds and races.

Churchill wrote to Nehru too. Only a few years before, in the middle of the war, Churchill had seen men like Nehru as Hindu "windbags" who at moments of crisis revealed "internal flabbiness".[36] Now he seemed to have noticed that Nehru had, like him, been to Harrow. Churchill grew so sentimental that he proposed that, even if India became a republic, in the style of republics in the Roman Empire, India could remain a republic within the Commonwealth and still accept the King. The monarch seemed to like the idea, and both men thought of the King becoming the President of India.

Nehru, who liked being described as the last English Prime Minister of India, was touched by Churchill writing to him and was in love with Edwina Mountbatten, the wife of Lord Mountbatten, Britain's last Viceroy. So, overriding fierce opposition from within his own Cabinet, he unilaterally changed a nearly twenty-year-old party policy and kept India in the Commonwealth. India, he decided, would become a truly independent country with its own President, but it would also remain part of a wider club – now no longer the old white man's club but one where other races could aspire to equality. India accepted "the King as the symbol of free association of its independent member nations and as such the head of the Commonwealth".[37] The King had no power in India, but became the permanent President of this new club – which also had no power.

This decision to keep India in the Commonwealth when its membership had no real significance is today being echoed in the Brexit debate about Britain's future relationship with the EU; in many ways it reflects the fact that, for all their reputation for being decisive and liking cut-and-dried solutions, the British have always believed that when it comes to disengagement there can never be a final goodbye. Ireland, Britain's oldest colony, provides the best example. The Irish Free State was formed by the Anglo-Irish Treaty of 1921, but independence was limited. So, Ireland could only send ambassadors in the name of the British monarch, which caused an enormous problem for it during the Second World War. Ireland was neutral, and had an embassy in Berlin but no ambassador: during the war a new ambassador could hardly be sent to Berlin in the name of George VI. It was only in 1949, two years after India got freedom, that Ireland officially declared itself a republic. Although Ireland refused to join the new multi-racial Commonwealth club that Nehru had helped create, no passport was required to travel between Ireland and Britain. And for all the political divisions and violence which have plagued the island, and despite Northern Ireland's fierce resistance to being part of the Republic in any shape or form, on the rugby field the two halves of the island are united. Here Northern Ireland players have no problem forsaking Britain and being part of the Ireland team. Moreover, while the Republic would never accept the British Crown – indeed, Irish Republicans do not even take their seats in the House of Commons as this would mean pledging allegiance to the British monarch – rugby players from Ireland happily form part of a team that for decades was called the British Lions (in recent years it has been renamed British and Irish Lions) and tour various parts of the world. During one such tour of Australia, the British national anthem was even played.

But perhaps the best post-war example of having your cake and eating it was the 1948 British Nationality Act, which Powell railed against. In many ways the 1948 Act can be seen as the model for the 1957 Treaty of Rome's provisions for free movement of labour, except that this free movement was not merely across Europe but, remarkably, all over the British Empire, even including parts of the Empire – like India and Pakistan – which had become free countries. Even more astonishing is the fact that Churchill and the Conservative Party inspired the idea. The Conservative manifesto on which Churchill fought the 1945 election had proposed that, in order to promote greater imperial integration, "movement of men and women within the Empire must be made easier":

A two-way traffic should grow. Those who wish to change their homes should be enabled to carry their national insurance rights with them wherever they go. Imperial ties should be knit together by closer personal contact and understanding.[38]

This is exactly the free movement that the EU has, and which for the Conservative Brexiteers is a red line that cannot be crossed. While the post-war Conservative manifesto did not specify who should be allowed to take part in the "two-way traffic", it was clearly understood as being meant to apply to whites going back and forth between Britain, Australia, New Zealand, Canada and South Africa – not brown people from the Indian subcontinent and black people from the Caribbean.

Indeed, there was post-war migration of white people from Britain to the "white" Commonwealth. Here we need to emphasise that, while Britain has taken in people from many lands, its historic role has been exporting rather than importing people. The normality of such migration is graphically illustrated in the final scene of the seminal post-war film *Brief Encounter*. The plot concerns the extramarital affair between Alec (played by Trevor Howard) and Laura (played by Celia Johnson), and ends with Alec emigrating to Johannesburg, where he has found a job. In real life, after the war many such Alecs did emigrate to South Africa, Rhodesia/Zimbabwe and, in even greater numbers, Australia. The latter had for decades followed a White Australia policy and in 1949 Arthur Calwell, the Minister for Immigration, made it clear that "there can be no half-measures in a matter such as the maintenance of the White Australia policy, on which Australians hold such emphatic views".[39] Australia saw the destruction caused by the war in Europe as a wonderful opportunity to get more Europeans to come and live down under. Australia particularly wanted the British. The "ten-pound Pom" policy – which subsidised the costs of travelling over from Britain – saw one and a half million white Britons migrate to Australia by 1982, when the policy officially ended.[40] These included Harold Larwood, an English cricketer that Australian cricket supporters had once hated, and three notable children migrating with their respective families: future high-profile businessman Alan Bond, and future Australian Prime Ministers Julia Gillard and Tony Abbott.

This wave of migration was matched by an even greater flow of brown and black people to Britain following the Second World War. By the beginning of the 1990s two million people had migrated from India, Pakistan, the Caribbean and Bangladesh.[41] This meant that after the war there had been an exchange of population in Britain based on colour. How big this change was can be judged if we go back to Orwell:

> It is quite true that the so-called races of Britain feel themselves to be very different from one another. A Scotsman, for instance, does not thank you if you call him an Englishman. You can see the hesitation we feel on this point by the fact that we call our islands by no less than six different names, England, Britain, Great Britain, the British Isles, the United Kingdom and, in very exalted moments, Albion. Even the differences between north and south England loom large in our own eyes. But somehow these

differences fade away the moment that any two Britons
are confronted by a European. It is very rare to meet a for-
eigner... who can distinguish between English and Scots
or even English and Irish.[42]

My experiences of meeting Europeans could not be more
different. Every time I say I am from Britain, they look at me
and say, "You cannot be British," and ask me where I really
come from. Likewise, recently Prince Charles met a woman
with Guyanese origins who said she was from Manchester,
and he responded, "Well, you don't look like it!"[43]

The post-war immigration of non-whites did raise a
great deal of concern, as shown by the minutes of a Cabinet
meeting on 3 November 1955:

If immigration from the Colonies, and, for that matter,
from India and Pakistan, were allowed to continue
unchecked, there was a real danger that over the years
there would be a significant change in the racial character
of the English people.[44]

Since then, changes to immigration policies have consistently
made sure that white Commonwealth citizens could come to
Britain unhindered. For example, the Commonwealth Immigrants Act 1968, which restricted non-white immigration, left
a loophole for white people, while the Immigration Act 1971
formalised their status by creating what were "patrials", those
with a British parent or grandparent. The Act did not have
to specify that the British ancestors had to be white, because
in that era they would almost certainly all have been white

in any case. Patrials had, and still have, the right to migrate to this country, and they can get a visa within three weeks of applying, while non-patrials must have work permits – which means having a job in this country waiting for them – and must also be sponsored by an employer.

As I write, the media is dominated by the saga of the so-called Windrush generation that arrived in the UK between 1948 and 1971 from Caribbean countries – many of whom migrated as children on their parents' passports and never applied for their own travel documents. Despite living here for almost half a century, these people's right to do so has now been questioned, and many of them have been threatened with deportation. Of course, had they been patrials, they would have had no such problem – but they are not. Much has been made of blunders at the Home Office leading to the landing cards of some of the Windrush generation being destroyed, which means there is no proof of when they entered the country. This sorry saga may be more than a case of British muddling and could be attributable to deeply concealed racism. My own personal experience is that the Home Office's decision making can be curious. In my case, this helped me become a writer.

In 1975, after six years' residence in Britain and having qualified as a chartered accountant, I was planning to leave this country for good. My parents had impressed on me that as their only son I had a duty to return home to India, and my brother-in-law had offered me a partnership in his accountancy firm: Indian nepotism married to old Aryan filial responsibilities. Before that, every year I sent my Indian passport to the Home Office and renewed my student visa.

But having, after much parental pressure, agreed to leave this country, suddenly one day my passport came back stamped: "You are allowed indefinite leave to remain." Now the only restriction on me was that I could not seek employment in Northern Ireland without asking for permission. That was understandable, as it was in the middle of the Troubles. I had not asked for it; I did not even know I qualified for such a privilege and, if truth be told, had given it no thought. It was as if this country had decided that, since I had lived here for six years, caused no trouble and decided to leave of my own accord, I deserved a leaving present. The wording was quaint, but then that is often how this country words momentous decisions. For example, during the First World War the Defence of the Realm Act was dubbed "DORA", to make a vital piece of legislation sound familiar and comforting. Now, this all-important question of which country a person was allowed to live in was phrased more like a case of a child being allowed a sleepover at a friend's house.

Today, such right to "indefinite leave" is not granted like an unexpected Christmas gift. A great deal of hard work has to be put in; lawyers must be consulted and books studied so the applicant can pass residency examinations that ask searching questions such as how many wives Henry VIII had. In 1975 it was different. There was no European Union, only a Common Market; the Berlin Wall had not collapsed – nobody expected communism in Europe to just vanish, let alone almost overnight; and millions of immigrants were not rushing in from eastern Europe taking jobs, or, as many allege, claiming benefits they were not entitled to. As an Indian I may not have been the most welcome of immigrants back in 1969, but by 1975 I had evidently earned my spurs for the Home Office to declare that this country was mine. The indefinite leave to remain I was granted meant that if I left the country I had to return within two years to preserve my residency. An Indian friend who had a similar right had dubbed this the new caste in Britain, the "Returning Residence" or "RR" caste, only in this case the caste mark was supplied not by a high Brahmanical priest but by the Home Office. For me this unexpected elevation to the new caste was to prove a boon. I had left the UK still nursing hopes to one day become a full-time writer. In India I had what my brother-in-law called "the good life" – cars, servants and so forth – but little opportunity to write. In 1978, when I returned to make sure I remained a member of the RR caste, the immigration officer, noticing I was merely coming back to stay in the caste, threatened me with expulsion from it. I decided that I did not want to lose my RR caste status. I would forsake India and the material comforts there and become a full-time writer in Britain. I have no doubts that, but for getting the unexpected Home Office present of indefinite leave to remain in the UK, I would never have fulfilled my dream. In Britain I could open doors. I even had lunch with one of my heroes, Neville Cardus, the legendary cricket and music correspondent of the then-*Manchester Guardian*, whose essay on the cricket superstar Ranji was part of my school English curriculum. I was a stranger, but Cardus readily agreed to meet me. In India a figure of Cardus's stature would have been surrounded by acolytes barring the door to a nonentity like me.

What makes the problems faced by the Windrush generation even more tragic is that while they may not have had the kinship that Australians had, they still saw Britain as a mother country. The family of Baroness Patricia Scotland, Secretary-General of the Commonwealth, came from Dominica, and she recalls:

> My mother and father had spoken of the United Kingdom as the mother country and my grandfather had fought during the First World War with Allenby and got three medals and people from the Caribbean felt they were very much part of the British diaspora, the British contingent. People from the Caribbean had come to Britain's aid in her hour of need during the war, now they had come to help the British rebuild their country. So, many people believed the experience they had during the war would be similar to the experience they would have on their return. They would be welcomed as British citizens coming to rebuild Britain. That wasn't the experience of people of my parents' generation. When we first came we lived in Paddington and it was very different to living in the Caribbean. My mother used to go to Mass every morning at six o'clock. She believed the UK would be a god-fearing country where people behaved properly and were decent. And she came to a London that was cold. That was dirty. We would bathe every single day, often three times a day. She found in this country nobody changed their clothes. They had public baths which people went to once a week. It was very different [to what she had imagined]. Those were the times when there were signs saying "no dogs, no Irish and no coloured". People were openly pejorative about black people.[45]

But even when shunned by the British, the West Indians clung to their concept of Britishness, for, as the West Indian writer CLR James, once a leading Trotskyist, put it, unlike the English, the West Indies lack "a national tradition" – a Drake, a Nelson, a Shakespeare or a Waterloo. Instead they have to use the West Indian cricket team playing the English game of cricket to represent "the whole past history and future hopes of the Island"; the cricketers help "to fill the huge gap in their consciousness and in their needs".[46] James' point is well made. There is no single West Indian nation; the cricket team, combining players from various islands often at loggerheads, brings together descendants of slaves taken to these islands far removed from their ancestral homelands.

These West Indians echo what Cardus once wrote:

> If everything else in this nation of ours were lost but cricket – her constitution and the laws of England of Lord Halsbury – it would be possible to reconstruct from the theory and the practice of cricket all the eternal English-ness which has gone to the establishment of that constitution and the laws aforesaid.

But no such thoughts of links with the "mother country" entered the heads of Britain's other wave of non-white immigrants. The bulk of the people who came from India, Pakistan and what is now Bangladesh had been ruled by the British, but few of them had ever met an English man or woman – there were very few Britons in India during the Raj. The overwhelming majority of these immigrants were not Christian, did not speak English and were not familiar with

British customs. This cultural distance illustrated the duality of British imperial rule: Britain had ruled these people, but had not embedded itself as part of their lives. I was made very aware of this a few weeks after my arrival in this country.

Not long after I was elected President of the Students' Union I received a message one day to contact a certain gentleman at Herbert Morris, the big local factory. It had for years employed a number of people from the subcontinent, but lately there had been some trouble with these workmen and they wanted somebody from their native land to come and help. This was my first visit to a factory site in England. It was like experiencing the world described by DH Lawrence in *Sons and Lovers*, with narrow, twisting cobbled streets leading to the immense factory gate. On either side of the gate were council houses, packed tightly next to one another with common walls and those peculiarly slanting English tiled roofs – and, most astonishing of all, outside toilets. I had been brought up to believe that in England every bedroom had an en-suite bathroom. All English houses in India had that, and well-off Indians aspired to have such English-style bedrooms.

Funnily enough, it turned out to be sanitation problems that had brought me to the Herbert Morris factory. I arrived to find that a group of workers had been assembled to meet me. They were from the eastern part of Bengal that was then Pakistan and is now Bangladesh. The foreman, a short, thick-set white man whose hands were constantly in the pockets of his soiled white apron, was clearly mortally embarrassed to talk about the problem. He started by saying that the men had been working for Herbert Morris for many years; that they were industrious, obedient, good; that they had never caused any problems. But now there was one.

He paused, took out his hands from his apron, rubbed them together and then, almost in a whisper, said, "You see, it's the loos. I mean, the loos are in such a condition now that the sweepers refuse to clean them. Well, as you must understand, one uses toilet paper in the loos. I realise some of the Bengalis were not accustomed to using toilet paper. They use water. As long as they keep it clean, it doesn't matter. But nowadays, in the loos, the sewage is found all over the place. Not just in the bowl but all over the floor. It's caused a tremendous problem. Could you help by talking to these people in their native tongue?"

As I began speaking to the workers in Bengali I realised that, like the foreman, I would have language problems. They spoke a Bengali dialect which I was not familiar with, and I had difficulty understanding them. I tried to explain the problem as best I could, and the workers nodded their heads.

Then one of them, a tall, well-built man, said, "Sir, we have been working here for many years. We know the customs of these people. It is true we do not use toilet paper, but we prefer to use water." He promptly turned to his machine and from somewhere behind it brought out a bottle of water. "We all have our own arrangements," he said. "We can assure you we have done nothing of the sort that has been alleged. We do not know who has done it." I emphasised to them the need to be very careful in their habits and manners and they all shook their heads in agreement. I translated the workmen's sentiments to the foreman, who put some questions through me to them. After that, it was agreed that I would write out a notice in Bengali which would be pinned to the noticeboard.

As I was about to leave, the tall worker who had acted as the spokesman for the group touched me on the arm and said, "Sir, we have been honoured by your visit. Will you please come and have dinner with us?"

"Yes," I said, "I would love to have dinner with you." I took down his address and said I would contact him so we could fix a day. But I never contacted the man whose address I had taken down.

Back then, I am ashamed to say, I did not want to know him, let alone explore the difficult journey those Bengalis had made. I have long since shaken off my Indian class prejudices and realised what an alien world they had come to in order to find work. They were not only alienated from the Windrush generation, but had come from remote, often rural parts of the subcontinent, with little or no exposure to the British in India.

One major group had come from an area which had not even been ruled by the British. These were Mirpuris from Kashmir, which during the British Raj was ruled by an Indian prince who had total internal autonomy. There, British laws were not applied, nor was British education imparted, and not even the legendary British railway had penetrated. In 1947, like the leaders of all princely states, the Kashmir ruler Hari Singh was given three options: join India, join Pakistan or stay independent. This incompetent Maharaja made such a mess of it that to this day both India and Pakistan claim Kashmir, and the dispute has resulted in two wars and ongoing military clashes between these former colonies. The

Mirpuris came from Pakistan-controlled Kashmir. The Bengalis were from Sylhet, a remote part of Bangladesh, far from the great metropolitan towns such as Dhaka. The Punjabis from India had had a bit more exposure to the British, but even they came from the rural part of the province. And they had come to a Britain in which, contrary to much modern myth-making, very few people had met someone born in India, as before 1947 there were very few Indians in this country.

It is against this background that these immigrants, particularly from Bangladesh, have achieved something that the British should be very proud of – even if it has meant deceiving the natives. The great majority of Indian restaurants in this country are run by Bangladeshis. Millions of native Britons go to these restaurants to eat what they consider to be standard Indian food. But it is not. For example, fish is a staple in the diets of the Bengali restaurant owners, and the great Bengali fish, hilsa, is full of lots of little bones. The Bengalis, like most people from the subcontinent, eat with their fingers and have no problem, but they were worried that the British, eating with knife and fork, would not be able to cope with the bones. So, with the help of their first cooks, Goan seamen, the dish they presented to the British as truly Indian was vindaloo, a speciality in Goa but unknown in the rest of the subcontinent. Vindaloo had no bones, and presented no problems for eating with a knife and fork. In other words, the Bengalis' restaurants did not serve the food they ate at home, a very interesting inversion of what you expect when you go out for a meal typical of a particular region.

The way these Bengalis have named their restaurants is

also ingenious. They have not used names from their home-land, realising they would not resonate here. Instead, they have given them names associated with India like "the Taj Mahal" or "the Raj" knowing it would make the British feel comfortable. This could not be more ironic. Back in 1947, when the subcontinent was partitioned, there had been a referendum in Sylhet to decide whether it would join India or Pakistan. Sylhet, whose residents are mainly Muslim, voted overwhelmingly to join Pakistan. But now, in Britain, their business dictates they advertise themselves as Indian. They have been so successful that chicken tikka masala – yet another concoction unknown in India – has become a British national dish. Had anybody suggested that to me in 1969 I would have considered it a fantasy.

Just as I did not foresee such a turn of events back in 1969, I also did not anticipate – and I doubt if many did – that another immigrant community's fortunes would go the other way and that in 2018 those people would be seen as a menace, contributing to the feeling of many people, like the Yorkshire farmer, that Britons had lost their country. These are the Poles, whose presence I was made aware of about the time I met my fellow Bengalis at Herbert Morris.

The lady I hired to type a thesis that I had to submit to my tutor looked no different to the great majority of white people I had met. But her surname did not sound English. It turned out her husband was a Polish man whose father had escaped to England after Poland was conquered by Hitler and had joined the Polish Royal Air Force, which flew alongside the Royal Air Force. To this Englishwoman it was no surprise that there were Polish people in this country, and for her it made no difference that she had a Polish surname. After all, Britain had gone to war to defend Poland against the Nazis, and many Poles had fled Hitler to come and fight with Britain on the side of the Allies.

This was also how Joanna Mludzinska, Vice Chair of the Polish Social & Cultural Association, felt until the Brexit vote changed things for her.[47] Her parents came to England after Hitler invaded Poland. They met in London and, after a wonderful romance, got married. There were also marriages in Britain between Britons and Poles, and, Mludzinska told me, "particularly in Scotland there were a lot of mixed marriages. These very gentlemanly Polish officers charmed the local ladies".

But when I met her after Brexit, she spoke sorrowfully of how the Polish Social & Cultural Association in west London was vandalised within days of the referendum result. She accepts that, unlike in 1969 when Britain's wartime alliance with Poland was recalled fondly, few now know about it, let alone care. "The younger generation see what they see," she says. "They see the Poles coming here to do these various jobs and that old association has gone." For her, the great struggle now is to make sure the Poles that are here do not lose their rights after Brexit. For Mludzinska this is the great moral argument about the Brexit debate. Britain went to war in 1939 not to seek territory but because it was morally right to come to the aid of a beleaguered country. Now, a majority in this country seem to want to forget their moral obligations to the Poles who have come to work in their country.

But then, Britain's desire to be always morally superior can take very strange forms. Consider the fact that this

country allows people from seventy-one countries and territories to vote in all the elections in this country, even if they
are not citizens. I first became aware of this extraordinary
voting arrangement during my first summer holidays, when
I worked for the council of the Royal Borough of Kensington and Chelsea. The pay was a generous £12 a week, which
went a long way, and the work was not very demanding. I had
to go from house to house in the borough distributing elec-
toral registration forms. The work produced some surprises:
Kensington and Chelsea, despite its reputation for being the
richest borough in the country, also had many poor residents.
Many of them had given up on politics, with some telling me,
"They're all the same, aren't they? Bloody politicians!" But
the biggest shock came when I read the form and discovered
that to register to vote you did not need to be a citizen of
this country. This very valuable privilege for which the British
had fought so long and hard has been extended to citizens of
the Commonwealth, British Overseas Territories and British
Crown Dependencies resident in this country – and this
right extends even to those on short-term visas. Even when
countries are suspended from the Commonwealth their citizens resident in Britain do not lose their right to vote in all
UK elections. This privilege includes three countries which
belong to the EU – namely Ireland, Cyprus and Malta – and
all because they were once part of the Empire. And yet, one of
them, Ireland, is not even a member of the Commonwealth.

This remarkable legacy of the Empire is little known and
arouses no resentment. Over the years, whenever I have
mentioned it friends have looked at me as if to suggest that I
must be mistaken. Despite Nigel Farage making so much of

ensuring EU citizens did not have a say in the Brexit referendum, he signally failed to mention that citizens of those three EU countries actually could vote in it. As for citizens of India, Pakistan, Bangladesh, Zimbabwe and Fiji voting, that clearly did not matter to him.

The most interesting reaction to these facts came at a forum just before the 2015 election. The three panellists were Michael Gove for the Tories, Ivan Lewis for Labour and Baroness Kramer for the Lib Dems. All three panellists made the point that they wanted immigration regulated fairly. So how did the panel react when I raised the issue of non-citizens voting? Lewis clearly disapproved of my broaching the subject and went on to say that some Conservatives had raised this issue, but it was a subject he felt should not be discussed. Gove did not rise to Lewis's bait and just said that he did not want to see any change in the franchise. Baroness Kramer justified retaining the present voting system on the grounds that the British do things differently. With that, she smiled. What I think Baroness Kramer was implying was that so many non-citizens being allowed to vote reflects the range and extent of the British Empire, and that, while the sun may have set on that Empire, the British still feel they have an obligation to the people from their erstwhile domains. In other words, the British cannot and do not want to forget their past, and this in a way allows them to occupy the moral high ground by showing how generous they are to people who come from their former colonies.

A British paradox: honouring defeat, not victory

The urge to always occupy a higher moral plane can also explain why the British, almost uniquely amongst nations, always honour moments of hardship or defeat and adversity in their history rather than their great victories. While there are no popular poems about great military victories such as Trafalgar or Waterloo, there is one about the Charge of the Light Brigade, which celebrates the bravery of a cavalry brigade charging in the wrong direction. The great battles of the First World War that defeated the Germans are hardly known and were little mentioned during the recent events to mark the centenary of the war, yet much was made of the four great disasters of that war: Mons, Ypres, Gallipoli and Passchendaele. Orwell saw this as a popular British distaste for fighting: "In England all the boasting and flag-wagging, the 'Rule Britannia' stuff, is done by small minorities. The patriotism of the common people is not vocal or even conscious."[48]

But while that may have been true of Orwell's generation, all the recent evidence suggests that now those who do not wave flags are likely to have their patriotism questioned, and that the British increasingly like to invoke their defeats to signify national cohesion and make the act of honouring them a proof of loyalty to the nation. This was well illustrated in the reaction to two much-acclaimed films of 2017, *Dunkirk* and *Darkest Hour.*

The Dunkirk evacuation is probably the one event of the Second World War everyone knows, and it is a classic case of the British nation coming together in its reaction to adversity. The film, released in the aftermath of Brexit, provided Nigel Farage with a wonderful opportunity to promote his great cause. After he saw the film he wrote on Twitter, "I urge every youngster to go out and watch #Dunkirk." This was accompanied by a photo which showed Farage standing stony-faced in front of a poster for the movie. His supporters immediately responded, one of them tweeting, "And if everyone watched this film, they'd probably understand why the majority of Britain voted for a FULL Brexit. No betrayal of our fallen!"[49] There were headlines in the pro-Brexit press such as "For Brexit to work, we need Dunkirk spirit not 'Naysaying Nellies'",[50] and there were reports that in cinemas there was applause when the scene was shown of an officer who, asked why he will stick it out on the bomb-strafed pier, replies with the word "hope". Similar pro-Brexit sentiments were also generated by *Darkest Hour,* which deals with the early days of Churchill's prime ministership. The film ends with Churchill's "fight them on the beaches" speech, and many cinemas reported audiences bursting into applause as Gary Oldman, playing Churchill, is shown making the speech. Journalist Ian Jack saw both films as suggesting "an England congratulating itself on its past – an idealised past, shorn of inconvenient fact... A film such as *The Cruel Sea,* made 65 years ago, gave my generation of children just as shocking an idea of what war meant, but refrained from a patriotic Elgar pastiche on the soundtrack (to which Dunkirk unfolds)".[51]

But if this suggests that the desire to appear morally right has increased over the years, both *Dunkirk* and *Darkest Hour* reveal historical distortions which suggest that the British, or certainly some of their film-makers, are going through a crisis of confusion when it comes to history. In real life, Indian soldiers and French Africans played a crucial part in the Dunkirk rescue, yet the film did not show any of them. Only white characters appeared, provoking much comment from Asians about how they continue to be written out of history. *Darkest Hour*, however, goes in the other direction. Churchill is shown in the summer of 1940 travelling on the Tube, asking the opinions of his fellow travellers and then quoting aloud from Thomas Macaulay's *Lays of Ancient Rome*. The verse is completed by a young black man, whose hand Churchill amicably touches. That is historical fiction. So why in one film is a real-life story of black and brown people forming part of Britain's very inclusive war effort excluded, yet in another a totally fictitious black man is imported into a Tube scene to suggest Churchill was inclusive when he wasn't? All peoples use the past to make sense of the present, but such ahistorical recreation of the past is nonsensical and damaging.

These are not the only films to tinker with history and in the process raise questions as to how our cultural opinion-formers want us to consider the past. For instance, in a recent remake of Agatha Christie's *Murder on the Orient Express* a black American character is introduced. He is in love with a white character, and is shown to resent the racial discrimination that prevailed in the US in the period of the film's setting. How this adds to the film is hard to say. The film also distorts how Christie dealt with different nationalities. She made Hercule Poirot, her ace detective, a Belgian (and a very proud one at that) who always corrects people who refer to him as French. She portrayed him as far superior to Chief Inspector Japp of Scotland Yard, who is often shown as a dimwit in contrast to Poirot, with his wonderful grey cells, who always solves every crime and often comes to the hapless Japp's rescue. For Christie, Poirot provides a wonderful chance to mock her fellow Britons. I can understand the desire to be inclusive, but to use Christie to do so is ridiculous.

More worrying is that Britain seems to be losing that capacity for self-examination that always made it special. The Second World War saw this country produce a collective effort it had never produced before. Yet during it there was no let-up of critical examination of the actions of the nation's leaders, not least Churchill. At the height of the war, Aneurin Bevan, then a Labour backbencher, while just as eager as Churchill to beat the Nazis relentlessly attacked the Prime Minister's war strategy. His most wounding jibe was that "The Prime Minister wins Debate after Debate and loses battle after battle".[52] Churchill was so angered by Bevan's attacks in the Commons that he called him a "squalid nuisance".[53] Many of Bevan's friends were also worried by his attacks. His friend Archie Lush asked him in anguish, "Why do you keep attaching Churchill? What do you think happens if he goes?" Bevan's reply was, "All right. Suppose he fell under a bus. What should we have to do? Send a postcard to Hitler giving in?"[54]

It is a reflection of how political life has changed that a modern politician would not dare make such a Bevan-style riposte. It is also hard to believe that in moments of crisis today the Commons would debate motions of no confidence. Churchill faced many such no-confidence motions during the war, and while he won all of them by massive majorities, there *was* debate. Now we have reached the state where any criticism of Churchill as war leader is seen as heretical if not downright unpatriotic. We are part of an age which has developed a sports-style discourse where tribal loyalty is everything, where your opponent is always your enemy and where you will never concede that he has anything good to say.

How this would have surprised Orwell. Consider how he begins his essay:

> As I write, highly civilised human beings are flying overhead, trying to kill me. They do not feel any enmity against me as an individual, nor I against them. They are 'only doing their duty', as the saying goes. Most of them, I have no doubt, are kind-hearted law-abiding men who would never dream of committing murder in private life. On the other hand, if one of them succeeds in blowing me to pieces with a well-placed bomb, he will never sleep any the worse for it. He is serving his country, which has the power to absolve him from evil.[55]

Can you imagine in the Brexit debate, where the issues raised are nothing on the scale of the Second World War, anybody on either side being so generous to their opponents?

I started by hoping that the farmer and his fellow Brexiteers who want their country back would not, like Powell, want to send me back to India. I have confidence in Britain: whatever the final agreement on Brexit, this country will go forward. But Britain needs to rediscover certain qualities which have always made it exceptional.

The British have always had a healthy scepticism, a refreshing ability to mock themselves. As George Steiner put it, only in English do you have the expression "What's your game, then?" This expresses the English horror of over-elaboration, mistrust of anybody trying to be too clever and aversion to anything that smacks of airy-fairy ideas with no practical meaning. It would be good to see the country rediscover this quality as it shapes up to its biggest decision for half a century.

Orwell ended his brilliant essay by saying that to win the war England had to be "true to herself... it is goodbye to the *Tatler* and the *Bystander,* and farewell to the lady in the Rolls-Royce car."[56] I wonder what Orwell would have made of seeing Meghan Markle arrive at church in a Rolls-Royce to marry into the royal family. It might have amused him to know that there is now in Parliament Square a statue of Gandhi behind that of Churchill. True, the Gandhi statue was erected because David Cameron wanted to court the people of Indian origin in this country, particularly the Hindus. But it was made possible by funds received from people all over Britain, showing that they had moved on from Churchill's belittling of Gandhi as a seditious lawyer posing as a half-naked fakir, a liar and a humbug. However, even if the masses can accept the lion sitting down with the lamb, there is yet little indication that, as we traverse the difficult and uncharted post-Brexit road, either the political class or the intelligentsia can.

Notes

1 Arthur Koestler, "The Lion and the Ostrich", *Suicide of a Nation?: An Inquiry into the State of Britain Today*, special issue of *Encounter*, July 1963, p. 5.

2 Ibid., p. 6.

3 John le Carré, *A Small Town in Germany*, New York, Simon & Schuster, 2002, p. 55.

4 George Orwell, *Collected Essays, Journalism and Letters, Vol. 2*, London, Penguin, 1971, p. 105.

5 Ibid., p. 107.

6 Ibid., p. 102.

7 Ibid., p. 119.

8 Ibid.

9 Ibid., p. 122.

10 Ibid., p. 113.

11 Ibid., p. 77.

12 Winston Churchill, *India*, London, Thornton Butterworth, 1931, p. 77.

13 George Santayana, *Soliloquies in England and Later Soliloquies*, Edinburgh, Constable & Co., 1922.

14 Richard Aldrich, *Intelligence and the War Against Japan*, Cambridge, Cambridge University Press, 2000, p. 133.

15 Pietro Quaroni, *Diplomatic Bags*, London, Weidenfeld & Nicolson, 1966, p. 110–15.

16   Orwell, op. cit., p. 79.

17   Milan Hauner, "One Man Against the Empire", *Journal of Contemporary History*, vol. 16, no. 1, January 1981.

18   Winston Churchill, *Frontiers and Wars*, London, Penguin, 1972, p. 118.

19   Ibid.

20   Nirad C. Chaudhuri, *Clive of India*, Bombay, Jaico Press, 1977, p. 465.

21   Ibid., p. 467.

22   Ibid., p. 469.

23   Jan Dalley, *The Black Hole*, London, Fig Tree, 2006, p. 198.

24   Chaudhuri, op. cit., p. 190.

25   William Dalrymple, *The Last Mughal*, London, Bloomsbury, 2006, p. 398.

26   Michael Edwards, *Red Year*, London, Cardinal, 1973, p. 59.

27   Niall Ferguson, *Empire*, London, Allen Lane, 2003, p. 153.

28   Afua Hirsch, *Brit(ish): On Race, Identity and Belonging,* London, Vintage, 2018, p. 29.

29   Ibid.

30   Orwell, op. cit., p. 79.

31   "Enoch Powell's 'Rivers of Blood' speech", *The Telegraph*, 6 November 2007, https://www.telegraph.co.uk/comment/3643823/Enoch-Powells-Rivers-of-Blood-speech.html (accessed 8 June 2018).

32   Ibid.

33   Ibid.

34   George Orwell, *Collected Essays, Journalism and Letters, Vol. 1*, London, Penguin, 1971, p. 434.

35   Ferguson, op. cit., p. 348.

36   Gabriel Gorodetsky (ed.), *The Maisky Diaries*, London, Yale University Press, 2015, p. 421.

37   Philip Murphy, *The Empire's New Clothes*, London, Hurst, 2018, p. 24.

38   CL Mowat, *Britain Between the Wars*, London, Methuen, 1956.

39   *I Stand By White Australia* [pamphlet], Arthur A. Calwell, Melbourne, 1949, p. 1.

40   Lisa Matthews, "The £10 ticket to another life", *BBC News*, 31 January 2008, http://news.bbc.co.uk/1/hi/magazine/7217889.stm (accessed 8 June 2018).

41   Ceri Peach, "Post-war migration to Europe: Reflux, Influx, Refuge", *Social Science Quarterly*, vol. 78, no. 2, June 1997, table 2, p. 274.

42   Orwell, *Collected Essays, Journalism and Letters, Vol. 1*, p. 83.

43   Bridie Pearson-Jones, "Ooops! The new Head of Commonwealth-elect Prince Charles told author with Guyanese roots who said she was from Manchester 'You don't look it!'", *Mail Online*, 20 April 2018, http://www.dailymail.co.uk/news/article-5638499/Prince-Charles-told-ethnic-minority-author-didnt-look-like-Manchester.html (accessed 8 June 2018).

44   CAB 128/29, CM 39 (55), minute 7, Cabinet meeting, 3 November 1955.

45   Interview by author with Baroness Scotland, London, 15 February 2017.

46 CLR James, *Beyond a Boundary*, London, Hutchinson, 1963, p. 225.

47 Interview by author with Joanna Mludzinska, 25 January 2017.

48 Orwell, *Collected Essays, Journalism and Letters, Vol. 1*, p. 80.

49 Christopher Hooton, "Nigel Farage is trying to make Dunkirk a Brexit thing", *Independent*, 26 July 2017, https://www.independent.co.uk/arts-entertainment/films/news/nigel-farage-is-trying-to-make-dunkirk-a-brexit-thing-a7860616.html (accessed 8 June 2018).

50 Allison Pearson, "For Brexit to work, we need Dunkirk spirit not 'Naysaying Nellies'", *Daily Telegraph*, 1 August 2017, https://www.telegraph.co.uk/women/politics/brexit-work-need-dunkirk-spirit-not-naysaying-nellies/ (accessed 8 June 2018).

51 Ian Jack, "Dunkirk and Darkest Hour fuel Brexit fantasies – even if they weren't meant to", *The Guardian*, 27 January 2018, https://www.theguardian.com/commentisfree/2018/jan/27/brexit-britain-myths-wartime-darkest-hour-dunkirk-nationalist-fantasies (accessed 8 June 2018).

52 HC Deb, 2 July 1942, vol. 381, c. 528.

53 HC Deb, 6 December 1945, vol. 416, c. 2544.

54 Michael Foot, *Aneurin Bevan: Volume 1: 1897–1945*, London, MacGibbon & Kee, 1962, p. 380.

55 Orwell, *Collected Essays, Journalism and Letters, Vol. 1*, p. 74.

56 Orwell, *Collected Essays, Journalism and Letters, Vol. 1*, p. 133.

ALSO IN THIS SERIES

The Power of Politicians (published with Westminster Abbey Institute)
by Tessa Jowell and Frances D'Souza

The Power of Civil Servants (published with Westminster Abbey Institute)
by David Normington and Peter Hennessy

The Power of Journalists (published with Westminster Abbey Institute)
by Nick Robinson, Barbara Speed,
Charlie Beckett and Gary Gibbon

The Power of Judges (published with Westminster Abbey Institute)
by David Neuberger and Peter Riddell

Drawing the Line: The Irish Border in British Politics
by Ivan Gibbons